Cool Millions

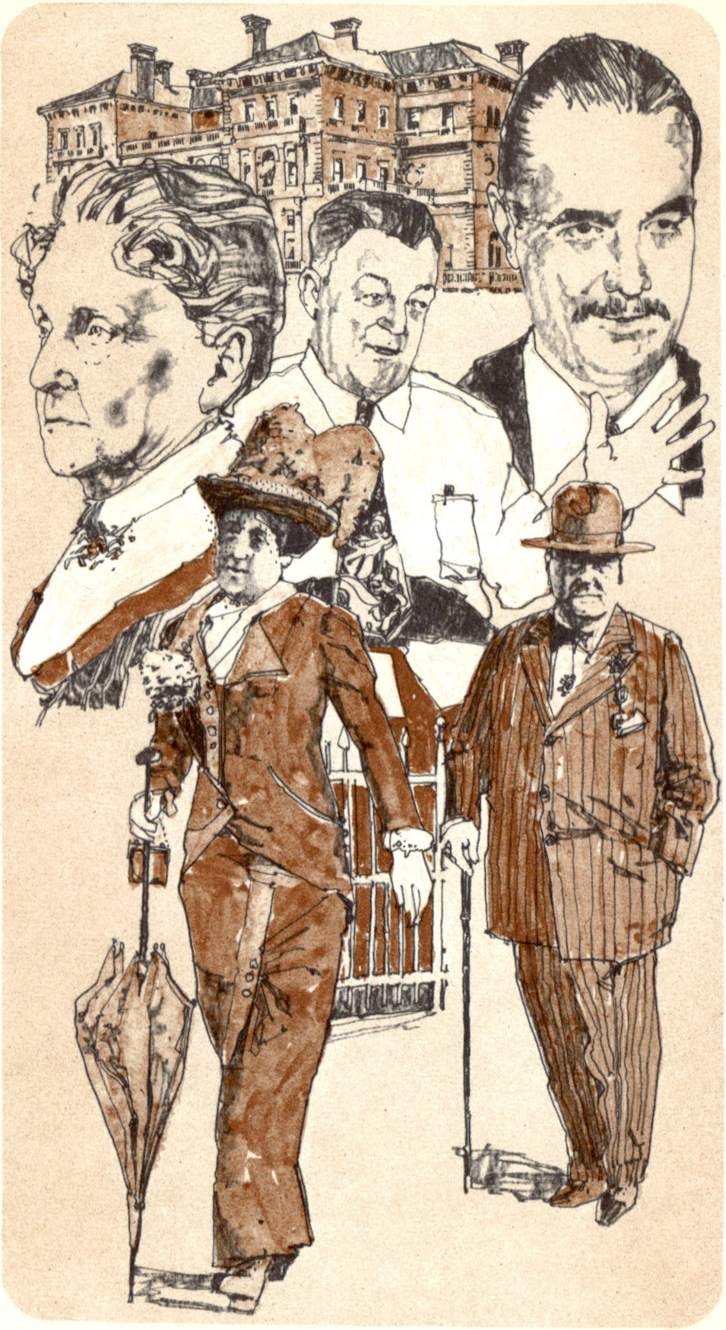

COOL MILLIONS
LIFE AMONG THE SUPER RICH

Edited by Robert A. Wood
Illustrated by Walter Scott

Hallmark Editions

"A 'Cottage' Called 'Breakers'" and "Laughing All the Way" from pp. 14-15 and 212-218 in *The Last Resorts* by Cleveland Amory. Copyright, 1948, 1952, by Cleveland Amory; copyright, 1951, 1952, by The Curtis Publishing Company. Reprinted by permission of Cleveland Amory. "The Only Way to Fly" from *Howard: The Amazing Mr. Hughes* by Noah Dietrich and Bob Thomas. Copyright ©1972 by Noah Dietrich and Bob Thomas. Reprinted by permission of Shirley Collier Agency. "Rx for Millions" taken from *Fads, Follies and Delusions of the American People* by Paul Sann. ©1967 by Paul Sann. Used by permission of Crown Publishers, Inc. "The World Is Mean to Millionaires" by J. Paul Getty reprinted with permission from *The Saturday Evening Post.* ©1965 The Curtis Publishing Company. "The Wicked Witch of Wall Street" from *The Day They Shook the Plum Tree,* ©1963, by Arthur H. Lewis. Reprinted by permission of Harcourt Brace Jovanovich, Inc., and Paul Gitlin, attorney in fact for Arthur H. Lewis. "The Golden Greek" reprinted by permission of Hawthorn Books Inc., and The Bodley Head from *Onassis: The Yachtsman Who's Had Them All Aboard* by Willi Frischauer. Copyright ©1968 by Willi Frischauer. All rights reserved. "King of the Gay White Way" from *Incredible New York,* by Lloyd R. Morris. Copyright 1951 Lloyd Morris. Reprinted by permission of Random House, Inc., and Nannine Joseph, agent for the Estate of Lloyd Morris. "Boy Wonder" from *Horatio Alger Is Alive and Well and Living in America* by David L. Goodrich. Reprinted by permission of Collins-Knowlton-Wing, Inc., and Henry Regnery Company. Copyright ©1971 by David L. Goodrich. "In America Anyone Can Become a Millionaire" in "From Bicycle Champ to Corporate Wheel" by John Peter Nugent. Copyright ©1972, Diners Club, Inc. Reprinted courtesy of *Signature* Magazine. "Profile of a Wheeler-Dealer" from "James J. Ling: Ling's the Name, Merger's the Game" in *The Young Millionaires* by Lawrence A. Armour. Copyright ©1973 by Lawrence A. Armour. Reprinted with permission of Playboy Press. Condensed from *Newsweek* article "Ling the Merger King." Copyright Newsweek, Inc., 1967, reprinted by permission. "Millionaire Housewife" from "Boss Tweedy: Lady With a Lot of Horse" by Martha Duffy in *Sports Illustrated* (June 11, 1973). ©1973 Time Inc. Reprinted by permission. "The Deuce With Love" from "The Deuce With Love and Advantage" by Robert H. Boyle in *Sports Illustrated* (August 28, 1972). ©1972 Time Inc. Reprinted by permission. Special research assistance by Kathleen Hoffine Saving.

Copyright ©1974 by Hallmark Cards, Inc., Kansas City, Missouri. All Rights Reserved. Printed in the United States of America. Library of Congress Catalog Card Number: 73-89442. Standard Book Number: 87529-383-2.

A man who has a million dollars
    is as well off as if he were rich.
John Jacob Astor I

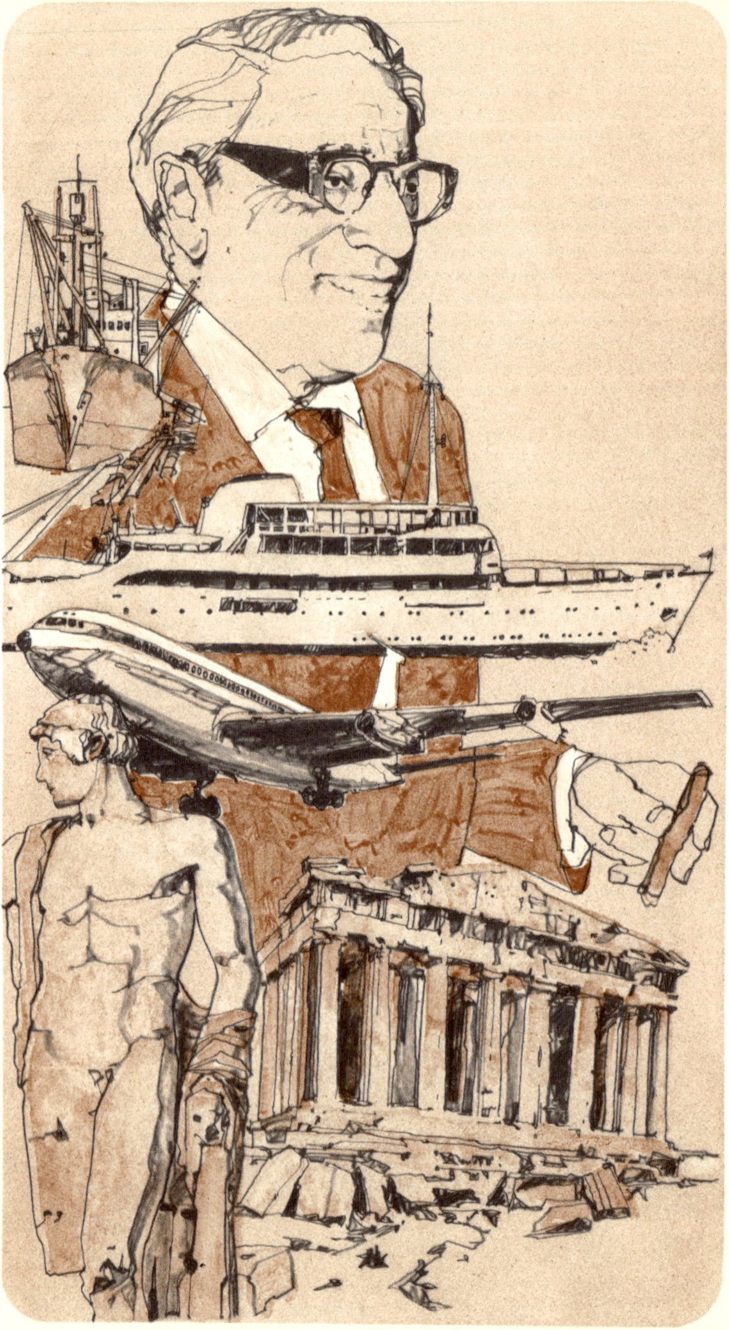

ARISTOTLE ONASSIS

The Golden Greek

There is nothing worse than a parsimonious millionaire. Aristotle Onassis is neither of the above. He is not stingy and he is not a millionaire. No, it is more nearly correct to say "zillionaire." From a private island to the world's costliest bathroom, Onassis has everything that money can buy.

Seven A.M. on a day in July, 1967. The sun is already high in the sky bearing down on Athens airport....But when his big, black American car sweeps through the gate, an 84-seat DC-6 airliner of Olympic Airways, which Onassis owns, is revving up to take its place.

After a 30-minute flight, he lands at Aktion, a desolate, lonely NATO airstrip on the western tip of the Greek mainland. A car is waiting—a car awaits Onassis wherever he goes—and soon rumbles along the stony, dusty road as fast as it can without crushing the passengers against sides or roof, but Onassis continues to study a batch of documents as if it were a small ride down Park Avenue. He does not look up until the car stops by a jetty where one of the *Christina's* speedboats is tied up.

Unceremoniously, he exchanges car for speedboat, which is off with a surge. For the first time the burden of business seems to fall from Onassis' shoulders. Standing up in his shirt sleeves at the back of the boat, he takes in the familiar, beloved view of the coast behind him and the islands ahead.... He drinks in the air as if craving the intoxicating properties of freedom.

In the distance is Ithaca, his spiritual home, but close by on the left lies Sparti, a tiny dot in the sea: "It's mine," he says, "I bought it as a protection against unwelcome neighbors." And now Scorpios, green, luscious, almost tropical, the 500-acre island shaped like a scorpion that Onassis bought in 1962 because he wanted roots in this part of the world....

Onassis steers his mini-jeep toward the quadrangle of new chalets that await his guests, each with bathroom, hot and cold running water and all modern conveniences, more than a dozen of them grouped around a big dining hall, with two very pretty maids in permanent attendance. On to the stables big enough for half a dozen horses, which can trot along the miles of riding paths he had cleared from the thicket.

The only snag is that after years of effort Onassis has failed to discover a source of water on the island, but three boatloads are brought in every day. Pipelines, part of a new seven-mile irrigation system, take the water to the reservoirs that have been built on the highest ridge. Gardeners use water lavishly to spray the flowers; Greek peasant women, heads covered with thick shawls against the relentless sun, water and prune the trees and strawberry bushes. The telephone exchange being completed ("Somehow it works by mirrors") is big enough even for the man whose lifeline is a telephone wire.

To the question, which of his residences he regards as his home — Avenue Foch in Paris, Alvear Avenue in Buenos Aires, Avenue d'Ostende in Monte Carlo, the house in Athens or Scorpios Island — Onassis has a prompt, unequivocal answer: "The *Christina*, of course!" He spends more time on his ship than in any of his homes, as much as four or five months a year, probably because it enables him to accomplish the impossible — to stay put and move about at the same time.... The crew of 50 ("More than it needs to run a 40,000-ton tanker," Onassis says, with a hint of self-reproach in his voice) have been busy sprucing her up after the Atlantic crossing. Now she is as finely polished and immaculate as when Onassis first took her over in 1954....

Onassis takes the dainty, vitrine-lined circular staircase to the bridge-deck and his private quarters, a three-room apartment. In the big study the shelves are filled with books — the collected works of Winston Churchill, each volume signed by the author with a big "W. S. C.," the English classics, the Greeks he likes best, Euripides, Herodotus, Plato; books on ships, on the arts, on Greece. He glances at the most precious of his paintings, El Greco's *Ascension* ("El Greco's El Greco," some of his friends quip), the Russian ikons, the swords in golden scabbards (a gift from Arabia's King Saud), and the whaling trophies on the wall.

Still dressed in his city clothes, he goes to the bedroom, almost sedate in this setting except for the 18th-century Venetian mirror and the gold-plated brushes, combs and containers of cosmetics, to the mirror-lined dressing room and the bathroom—ah, the bathroom! For years it has been a talking point among millionaires, because there is nothing quite like this Sienna marble temple—the bath itself an exact replica of the one in King Minos' lost Palace of Knossos in ancient Crete, with inlaid flying fish and dolphins of delicate beauty made by mosaic artists in Berlin. But even here he is soon on the telephone—three of the *Christina's* 42 extensions are in the owner's quarters.

While he changes into a pair of brown slippers and white linen trousers, leaving his muscular, sun-burned torso bare, his guests—the president of an oil company, an international banker, an American insurance tycoon with families and friends, owners of no mean yachts themselves — wander through the *Christina* like reverent visitors in the Museum of Modern Art....Onassis takes his guests to the poop deck and the huge, elegant smoking room with its grand piano and the open fireplace of lapis lazuli, which cost four dollars a square inch.

Before lunch, the more venturesome guests are encouraged to join their host in a swim of some 200 yards to one of Scorpios' soft, pebble beaches. Onassis makes this swim twice every day, striking out vigorously with the stamina of a man half his age. The party naturally gravitates toward the bar, which is also unique. Genuine old parchment maps line the walls, tiny models of almost every famous ship from Noah's Ark to the Kon-tiki are under glass. The bar stools are covered with white whaleskin, and giant whale teeth serve as support for those who do not find their sea legs at once. Onassis, who takes quite a few whiskies in the evening, prefers an iced Coke during the day....

Then comes the call to lunch, prepared by the French chef (a Greek chef caters for those who prefer native cuisine): freshly caught prawns, Macaroni à la Béchamel, roast veal, local goat cheese, ice cream, fruit, pink champagne, Turkish coffee, liqueurs and brandy. Onassis offers cigars of

Churchillian proportion, and lights one himself.

Afterward, the guests return to the cabins for a siesta—nine double cabins along the corridor below, each named after a different Greek island, each a gem of luxury designed in a different style, with baths, showers, washbasins with fish-mouth faucets, lavatories and bidets of different-colored marble....

After the siesta the men gather for a drink. The talk of this In-group of wealth, power and influence is deliberately inconsequential, but the calls over the radiotelephone and the cables and messages from the other yachts, brought in on silver trays, keep the spirit of "big business as usual" alive under the nonchalant surface....

And so Aristotle Socrates Onassis goes on and on like the sea he loves so well—surrounded simultaneously by mystery and headlines, by fascinating women and financial transactions involving fantastic sums of money.

From time to time, he finds himself exposed to the question that pursues every wealthy man: "How does one become a millionaire like you?"

To this question, Onassis has given a classic answer—one that sums up his own fabulously successful life: "One must always swim on top," he says, "like oil!"

HETTY GREEN
The Wicked Witch of Wall Street

Hetty Green, through forgery, perjury, penury, ruthlessness and stamina, built one of the largest fortunes in history, but lived as a pauper. She fashioned old newspapers into underclothes. She divorced her husband when he lost his money, saying, "He is a burden to me." Here Arthur Lewis explains further why most people detested Hetty Green.

Hetty's days were spent on Wall Street and behind a desk that the Seaboard National Bank gave her at 18 Broadway. Frequently, officials of that institution must have wondered if the business they got from Mrs. Green was worth the trouble she caused them.

First of all, Hetty was visible from the main lobby and this brought in more curiosity seekers than depositors. Then, too, she rarely bathed. Since she wore the same inner and outer garments for long periods without a change or wash, the combined bouquet that was wafted to nearby desks must have been less than fragrant.

Hetty also insisted on bringing her own lunch and eating it in the presence of employees and customers....She was a firm believer in the efficacy of hot oatmeal. A huge bowl of this cereal, which cost a fraction of a cent per serving since Hetty ate it dry, would, in Mrs. Green's own words, "give me the strength I need to fight those Wall Street wolves."

The Seaboard, like most institutions of its day, was heated by a system of ventilators, which provided no place for Mrs. Green to warm the large tin of oatmeal she brought from Hoboken every day....She solved her problem by using the facilities of a nearby broker, Stephen T. Kelsey, whose son, Stephen T. Kelsey, Jr., recalls Hetty's prompt arrival in the office each morning.

..."Each morning I used to see an old, dowdy-looking woman, dressed in a long black, trailing skirt, come in and deposit a covered pail on our radiator. She'd pat my head, then speak to my father for a few minutes and leave. She'd return at noon, say hello to the clerk, take the package off the radiator, and go out again.

"I used to think she was some unfortunate creature in to ask my father for a handout. Well, one day I asked our clerk who the lady was and what she was warming on our radiators.

"He laughed. 'That's Hetty Green,' he told me, 'and what she's heating on our radiators is oatmeal. I don't know how she eats the stuff when summer comes.'"

But the worst annoyance the Seaboard had to endure was, strangely enough, Hetty's large

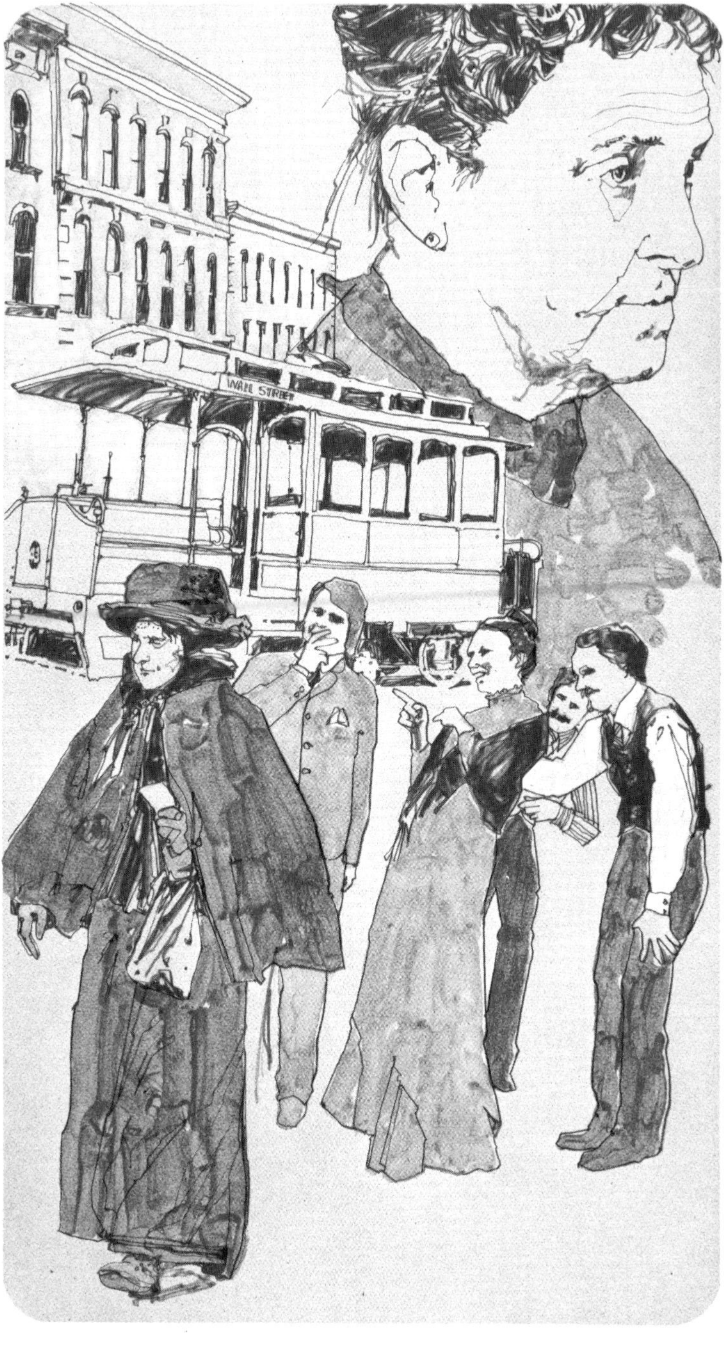
WALL STREET

amounts of surplus cash.

"We were only a medium-sized bank in those days," an official said, "and you'd have thought we'd have welcomed the big deposits Mrs. Green made with us. But it wasn't worth a thing. All it did was take up space. We couldn't invest it; we couldn't lend it even on short-term notes. No! It made us uneasy and Hetty knew it.

"There were times when she'd have as much as thirty million dollars lying around for a month.... The money *had* to be on hand at all times. There wasn't a morning or afternoon when Hetty wouldn't walk over to the first teller's cage and say, 'Joe,' or 'John,' or 'Bill, I might need all my money today.'"...

Hetty was then in the midst of more concurrent litigation than even she was accustomed to handling. She was suing one New York brokerage firm for what she claimed was the mishandling of her funds and was, in turn, being sued by a Wall Street operator for failure to pay his commissions....

Hetty did better in Boston. There, the case against her was dismissed, but not before the defendant scared the wits out of the plaintiff, the dignified Joseph Choate, a member of the New York Bar.

Because she claimed to be afraid of robbery, Hetty was granted permission to carry firearms.

In her case this meant a small-caliber revolver which usually reposed in her large handbag.

Mr. Choate, a youthful victim of a hunting accident, lived in deathly fear of firearms. The sound of a distant rifle shot could send this lawyer, bold enough in the courtroom, into whimpers. Hetty knew this. She made sure that, soon after the trial opened, Boston newspapers carried stories not only of Hetty's ownership of a pistol but also her prowess in its use.

John McMahon, on the staff of the Boston *Herald* and an expert on the Green family, recalled Hetty's day in court.

"There was a heavy drizzle," he said, "and the session had already begun when Mrs. Green entered, carrying a big umbrella. She went directly in back of Mr. Choate, the enemy, bustled about somewhat, shook her wet jacket on his hair, uttered a stage-whispered threat or two, and sat down loudly.

"With the exception of Mr. Choate, who ignored her completely, everyone in the crowded room, including His Honor, either was grinning or restraining a smile and anticipating a cheerful break in an otherwise dull trial. Hetty did not disappoint them.

"A bit later she was called to the box. There was a moment of silence during which all eyes turned to Mrs. Green. It was then that she raised her umbrella, pushed its point into Mr. Choate's back, and rapidly clicked the spring on it six times in succession as though she were loading her revolver. Mr. Choate gave a cry of terror, leaped out of his chair, and dashed to the comforting presence of a bailiff. Only after the howls of glee had died down and the Judge rapped for order, did Hetty take the stand."

PENNY TWEEDY
Millionaire Housewife

Meet Mrs. Penny Tweedy—millionaire. She's the boss of Meadow Stables, home of Secretariat, the first horse to win racing's Triple Crown in twenty-five years. In a recent interview, Martha Duffy found that Penny is as much housewife as turf pro.

It is eight o'clock on a clear spring morning at The Meadow farm, a 2,600-acre breeding establishment in the unfashionable reaches of Virginia. Penny Tweedy, who runs it, has carved time from her schedule for the important business of showing her track trainer, Lucien Laurin, the yearling crop and the laggard 2-year-olds who are not already in Laurin's Belmont barn learning how to get out of a starting gate.

The yearlings have already passed in a slow parade of inspection—Somethingfabulous, king of the barn, a Northern Dancer-Somethingroyal colt already worth about $300,000; Line Officer, a deep-chested son of Crewman; a Dr. Fager filly whose legs are causing concern; and eight other glistening animals.

The party moves on to the training track to examine the 2-year-olds. Mrs. Tweedy knows their problems right down to Tally Round, a particularly intractable filly who tries to swallow her tongue, paddles when she walks and generally resists direction.

"Have her teeth been filed yet?" the owner asks. Just then a buzzer sounds indicating a phone call. It is her husband Jack back home on Long Island. Where are his shirts, he wants to know.

That problem dispatched, Mrs. Tweedy tells her farm trainer, Meredith Bailes—whose father worked at The Meadow for 25 years—that she wants to buy a starting gate to train her own horses as well as others on consignment. Before she invests, she wants Bailes to spend two or three months away from the farm in intensive training with Laurin. Bailes looks as if he has heard better ideas in his time, but the plan will probably go through.

In the six years since she took over the management of Meadow Stud from her father, the late

Christopher Chenery, Mrs. Tweedy has cut the stable's size from 130 horses to 68, mostly eliminating dead wood. The overall plan is to tighten the operation in every way possible.

Mrs. Tweedy is the most visible owner in racing in a long time, and the closest thing to a new face that settled Establishment has. In manner and life-style she is considerably removed from more flamboyant racing ladies, such as Elizabeth Arden. Penny Tweedy is practical and energetic, as careful with time as with The Meadow budget. When giving an interview she may be sewing on buttons. On Long Island her only help is a part-time secretary and a cleaning woman. Jack's shirts and Tally Round's teeth are coexisting responsibilities.

In May, 1900, at the age of three months, John Nicholas Brown became the world's richest baby when his father and uncle died within a few months of each other leaving him sole heir to two multimillion dollar fortunes. Brown grew up at "Harbour Court," Newport, a dark, Victorian feudal castle, where he was literally tied to his governess — bound, from her wrist to his, by a blue silk cord and surrounded by guards. He had only one playmate, a friend named "Akerbodie" whom he made up.

JAMES HENRY VAN ALEN

The Deuce With Love

Who wants to revitalize baseball by eliminating the shortstop and center fielder? Who proposed to add interest to the America's Cup yacht races by starting the boats 100 yards above Niagara Falls? James Henry Van Alen, that's who. And now he's after tennis.

By his own definition, James Henry Van Alen, a millionaire sportsman of 69 who looks like a cherub, is "a busy little body." He has been called "the first gentleman of Old Guard society in America" and "Newport's last *grand homme*," and, given his money and position, Van Alen could have been just another social gadabout, but he is driven by an almost manic spirit of *noblesse oblige*. In his efforts to make the world a better place than he found it, Van Alen has espoused the cause of Santa Claus, put up the money to rescue the journals of James Boswell from Malahide Castle in Ireland, edited the *North American Review*, rejuvenated the Soldiers', Sailors' and Airmen's Club in New York, saved the landmark Newport Casino, collected the greater bustard and other rare Iberian birds for the American

Museum of Natural History and promoted the reformation of scoring in tennis with such fervor that he was recently given a new sobriquet, "the Rolls-Royce radical."

Of all his interests, Van Alen is most intense about tennis. A tournament player in his younger days, he says, "I don't want you to think I'm a nut, but tennis established me *on my own.*" As far as Van Alen is concerned, millions upon millions of people should be playing tennis regularly, but in his opinion the sport will never achieve the great popularity it deserves as long as matches drag on and the scoring is obscured with terms such as "love" and "deuce," pseudoarchaic words imposed on tennis, Van Alen says, by the English in 1873.

In line with this Van Alen, who turns out verse on any subject that engages him, has written a poem, *The Facts of Love*, which goes in part:

> The French think English crazy
>   For the way they score at tennis —
> To claim that 'love' means nothing
> To a Frenchman makes no sennis.
> "Love all" the English umpire cries,
>   And means a double zero;
>   What more's required to prove
>   The English thinking's out of gear-o?

It's true that 'l'oeuf' means 'egg' in French,
And sounds like 'love' in English;
But Frenchmen claim a moron should
Be able to distinguish;
For love is love the world around
And zero's always zero,
And they who claim they mean the same
Must be a trifle queer-o.

To reform tennis Van Alen has thought up the Van Alen Simplified Scoring System, known as VASSS. In VASSS zero replaces the term love, and deuce and advantage are eliminated entirely. Briefly put, individual games are simply scored one, two, three instead of 15, 30, 40, and the game goes to the first player who wins four points....

As the result of devising VASSS, Van Alen is convinced that his name will go down in history. "Pasteur pasteurized milk, I will VASSSify tennis," he says.

―――※―――

During the first decade of this century wealthy James Stillman achieved the ultimate in indoor plumbing when he installed a waterfall in his dining room.

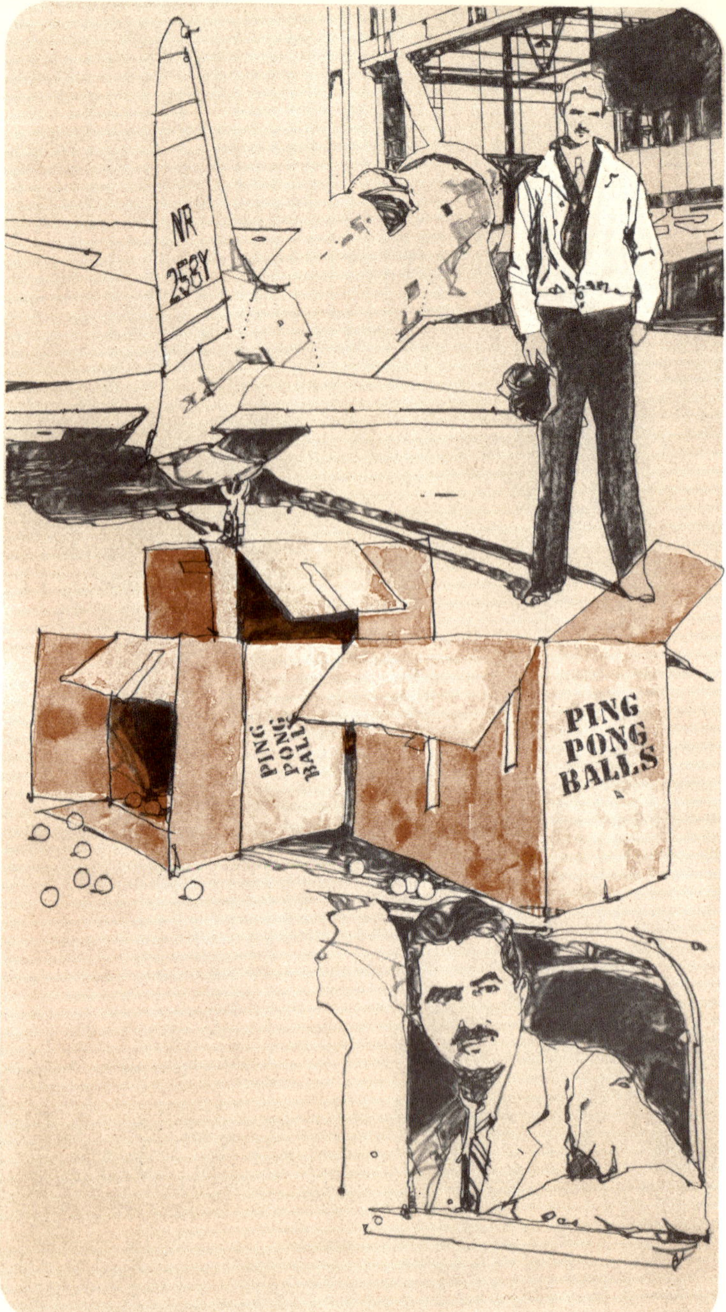
NR 258Y
PING PONG BALLS
PING PONG BALLS

HOWARD HUGHES
The Only Way to Fly

Billionaire Howard Hughes once stated his intention "to be the greatest aviator in the world." He realized his dream in 1939 when he broke Wiley Post's round-the-world flight record. He did it in typical Hughes style, packing along a shotgun, a kite, a picnic lunch and eighty pounds of Ping-pong balls. His associate, Noah Dietrich, recalls the unique ninety-one-hour trip.

The first I knew about Howard's plan to fly around the world was when he invited me out to his hangar to look at the Sikorsky amphibian he had bought. He had removed all the seating arrangements and had installed two rows of large gas tanks. These tanks extended from the roof to the floor and held about 200 gallons each....

Later he decided the Sikorsky wasn't fast enough, and he bought a Lockheed Lodestar. Again he had the plane stripped down to its shell and fuel tanks were installed. He devised a new fuel system, coating the tanks with neoprene to make them self-sealing.

Howard had first wanted the Sikorsky amphibian because he wanted to be able to land safely on earth or water. The Lodestar was a land plane, but Howard devised a means which would allow it to float.

"I've put eighty pounds of Ping-pong balls in every recess of this plane," he told me. "So even if I rip off a wing landing in the ocean, it'll still float."...

Howard left absolutely nothing to chance. He took along everything that he might possibly need—a shotgun in case he crash-landed among unfriendly beasts; a solar still to convert sea water to fresh; a kite to fly a radio antenna; parachutes with small radio transmitters. He carried ethyl to mix with ordinary fuel in case he couldn't find the kind he needed along the route. He even tested thirty different breads for nutritive value, to be used in the crew's sandwiches....

The Lodestar was ready for takeoff from Floyd Bennett Field on July 10, 1938. Howard had made a tie-up with New York officials and had named the plane *New York World's Fair, 1939.* There were departing ceremonies with speeches by Mayor Fiorello La Guardia and Grover Whalen, the famed greeter and president of the World's Fair. Howard was happy when the speeches were over and he could climb in the Lodestar and take off.

He almost didn't make it. Sagging under its heavy load, the plane rumbled down the runway and into a field—Howard had prudently ordered the fence removed. Finally the Lodestar rose above the cloud of dust and nosed eastward....

The whole world was keeping track of the *New York World's Fair, 1939*, as it flew over the Bering Sea and landed at Fairbanks. There he was greeted by Mrs. Wiley Post, widow of the flier whose record Howard was beating.

The Lodestar flew on, bypassing the scheduled stop of Winnepeg because of a storm and landing in Minneapolis. The last leg of the flight was the most hazardous. The plane ran into a hailstorm, and the wings shook under the bombardment of hailstones. Howard lowered the speed almost to the point of stalling and managed to escape the storm without damage.

A huge crowd had assembled at Floyd Bennett Field by the time the *New York World's Fair, 1939,* touched down. The reception led by Mayor La Guardia and Grover Whalen dissolved into chaos as the idolatrous mob clamored for the handsome young air hero, Howard Hughes.

In 1972, Robert H. McIntosh of Winter Park, Florida, died leaving the American government over $1 million. McIntosh was a childless widower who spent his last years in a modest boarding house. He made the bequest because he wanted to show "my appreciation to my country."

MILAN PANIC

In America Anyone Can Become a Millionaire

What becomes of the countless refugees who have escaped from iron curtain countries to come to America? One—Milan Panic—became a millionaire. He and his wife escaped from Yugoslavia in 1955. They arrived in this country with $20. Panic started a pharmaceutical company in his basement. Today he is worth over $6 million. Reminiscing here with John Peter Nugent, Panic talks about his days as a Yugoslav freedom fighter and the good life he has found in his new homeland.

The nabobs of Pasadena are often the subject of jokes that have to do with the idle pastimes of the idle rich. But among the coupon clippers of this affluent Southern California community, there is no joke and nothing whatsoever idle about a millionaire with the improbable name of Milan Panic (pronounced Pon-nish), a one-time Yugoslav freedom fighter and national 1,000-meter bicycle champion.

Still trim as in his bike-racing days, the 42-year-old Serbian is almost literally a study in perpetual motion as he runs the world-spanning organization he founded in 1960—a health-care complex called International Chemical & Nuclear

Corporation. The company produces and distributes pharmaceuticals and it manufactures biochemicals and radioactive materials. ICN's 1971 sales were $135,700,000—up a vigorous 17 percent over 1970. The $300,000-a-year executive (whose shares in ICN are currently worth $6 million) sports the tricorn of chairman, president, and chief executive officer. He oversees a drug empire of 4,900 employees organized into 20 divisions in 14 countries of the world. His 1,000 salesmen crisscross 110 different nations with a product list that runs from lyophilized (freeze-dried) viper venom to L-dopa, a controversial "wonder drug" for the treatment of Parkinson's disease. The company, a rising David among a field of Goliaths with names like Upjohn and Eli Lilly, is listed on the New York Stock Exchange—happily, its employees like to point out, right below IBM....

On a recent afternoon, Panic silently weighed such factors as the probable local resentment to an American firm buying up a Munich drug house, the stability of a labor force in western Brazil, the domestic consumption of drugs in South Africa. He ordered one "go" and two "no go's," then instructed his polylingual Dutch secretary to call the Burbank airport to alert the flight crew for a quick trip to Mexico City in his 10-place Lockheed Jet Star, a machine that he uses like a telephone. Now turning to a visitor he said, in his engaging East European accent: "Reason to make money is to contribute something. We like to produce medicine. I want more medicine for less money. I am concerned with how we live in America."...

"I saw people hung in streets of Belgrade," he recalled. "We would go by in streetcars that hit legs of those hanging from light posts."

Gradually the full story emerged.

As a teen-ager Panic had been a courier for Partisan forces fighting in the mountains against Hitler's troops. Then the war ended and the fight for freedom that had engaged a young man's patriotism transformed into something ugly and restrictive. The country was gripped by Communism.

Panic began the study of science in Belgrade. He married a fellow student. Finding their life in Yugoslavia increasingly distasteful, they plotted together to get out of the country, and dreamed of somehow reaching the United States....

Panic speaks repeatedly of his sense of opportunity and of its importance in the American way of life. "When you have no experience with something is difficult to understand," he says. "*You* read about Communism in books. *I* have lived under it."

But it should be made clear that Panic is no

flag-waver of the radical Right. He was a strong financial backer (and is still a good friend) of Senator Birch Bayh when that Indiana Democrat was in the Presidential race. He was a contributor to Senator Edmund Muskie's campaign for the same elusive mantle. In fact, Panic's view is more empirical than partisan. He is simply convinced that America is by far the best country in the world to live in.

"It is place where problems are resolved," he says...."Americans have to be more conscious of our values. We do bad public relations job. There is failure to convey America to world. Yes, we have racial problems. But Angela Davis was freed."

He pauses to sip from the tall white ICN coffee cup which he keeps on a coaster in a desk drawer.

"Before I come here, I used to read it was very competitive country," he continues. "But competition is all right when you have opportunity. To be millionaire in Communist country, you've got to be president of country. Here anyone has opportunity to become millionaire."

GLADYS VANDERBILT

A "Cottage" Called "Breakers"

"The rich have many consolations" said Plato in The Republic. *Doubtless his remark ranks as one of the classic understatements of all time. One need only read this account of a modest cottage on the other side of the tracks. Some consolation!*

The real "Breakers" at Newport, the most famous resort cottage ever built in this country, was built in 1895. In 1948 it was leased by its owner, Countess László Széchényi, the former Gladys Vanderbilt, to the Newport Preservation Society for the sum of one dollar and opened to the public. Today... a visitor can see a cottage which cost five million dollars in the days when a million dollars was a million dollars and could not now be duplicated for twenty million dollars. Designed by Richard Morris Hunt, who made a specialty of turning foreign palaces into American cottages, and vice versa, "The Breakers" boasts an ornamental wrought-iron fence outside which currently costs over five thousand dollars a year just to keep painted. The front doors—there are two sets of double doors even after you get by the outside gate—are no come-ons either; one set weighs

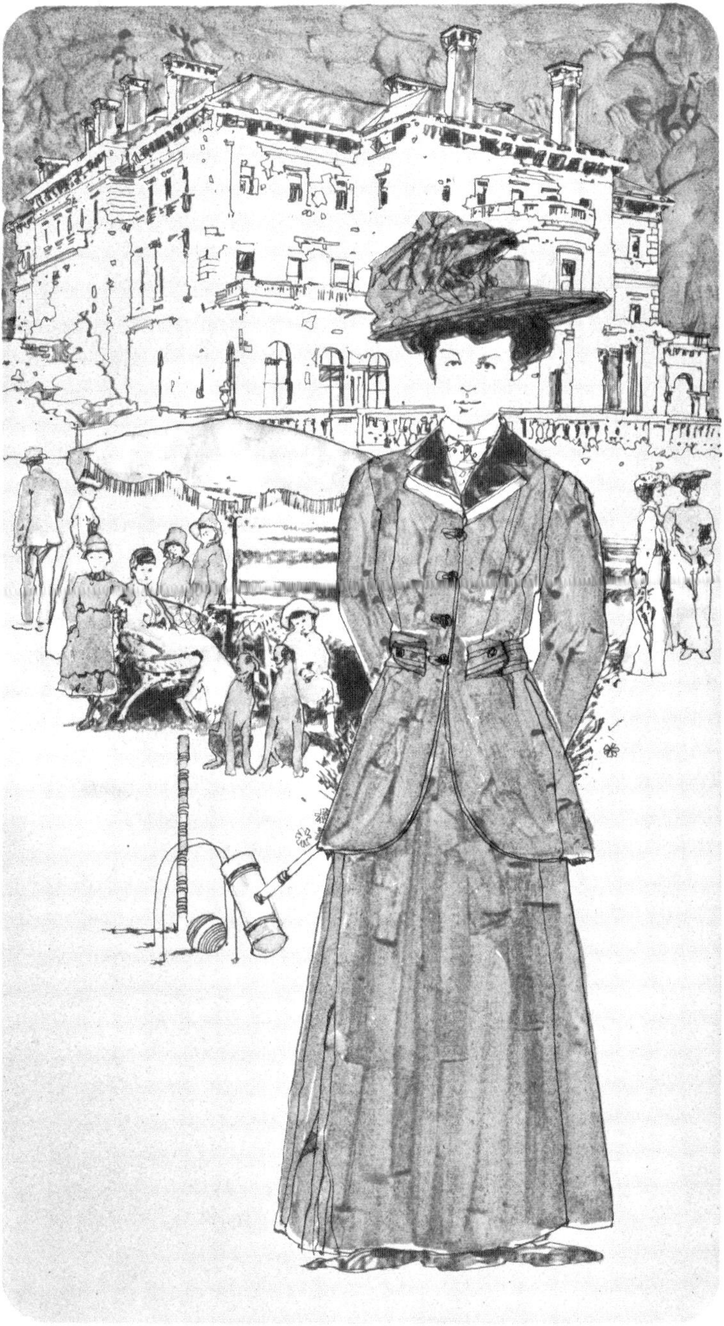

seventy tons. In the entire cottage, in order to insure a completely fireproof building, not a single stick of timber was used; the chandeliers are both wired for electricity and piped for gas, and the bathrooms are fitted with outlets for both hot and cold salt, as well as fresh, water. Four floors and a total of seventy rooms (thirty-three of them for servants) center around a monumental hall which rises over 45 feet through two floors to what is undoubtedly the most breath-taking interior of any house—let alone cottage—ever built in this country. The dining room, which is covered by a distant ceiling painting of Aurora at Dawn, has been called more ornate than any single room in any palace abroad, and even the Billiard Room, in which the walls are faced from floor to ceiling with matched slates of pale gray-green Cippolino marble, is by no means to be confused with a rumpus room.

Tourists often overlooked this cottage's motto; this is engraved in French over the library fireplace. Translated, it reads: "Little do I care for riches, and do not miss them, since only cleverness prevails in the end."

MIKE CURB
Boy Wonder

A most unusual talent who got his start in bubble gum music and trend songs like "You Meet the Nicest People on a Honda," Mike Curb is conceded to be something of a boy wonder. After all, few people drop out of school to become millionaires. Mike Curb did, and here David Goodrich tells his story.

When I interviewed Mike Curb—a cherub-faced early-Beatle-haired twenty-five-year-old who founded his own music company at nineteen, sold it for $3 million when he was twenty-two, and then, at twenty-four, became the $100,000-per-year president of MGM Records, in which capacity he controlled several hundred employees, had masterminded a crash program to update and salvage a troubled operation, and jetted regularly from continent to continent making deals—he was asleep. Not dead to the world, one hundred percent asleep, it's true, but close. He punctuated his talk with gaping yawns; his lids kept fluttering down over his gray-green eyes; he kept sagging in his leather-padded swivel chair, then jerking himself erect. We were in an office in MGM's New York outpost, a mid-fifties office tower (the company's headquarters were in Los

Angeles), and Curb apologized for and explained his condition:

"I'm telling you, that all-night flight really puts me out. It leaves L.A. at eleven, and gets here at six-thirty in the morning, and you wonder what happened to the night. Last night, I was surrounded by people who were chattering, so I didn't sleep at all. I came straight here from the airport. This afternoon, I'm flying to London and then, the day after tomorrow, to Germany. I've made dozens of trips across the country and abroad since I joined MGM, in December '69, and I don't enjoy them at all. They're too hectic. I like to stay in one place."

He shifted his heavy-lidded gaze to a No-Doz pill resting beside a glass of water on the desk. "My secretary gave me that to wake me up, but I'm afraid of it. So you'll have to excuse me."

The first impression you get on meeting Curb is of carefree, youthful casualness; he has all the earmarks of an easy-going, well-mannered teenager, who has temporarily put aside his surfboard to play executive. The face and haircut contribute to the feeling; so does an informal, but deferential, conversational style. After asserting something, he's apt to pause, and ask, "Isn't that so?" or, "Wouldn't you agree?" I kept waiting for him to call me "Sir."

In addition, on the morning of our talk, he was

dressed almost sloppily, in tan slacks and a robin's-egg-blue turtleneck. (I gathered that coming directly from the airport had something to do with that.) Finally, he is put together like (there's no other word) a kid—tall, thin, narrow shoulders, loose joints—and he doesn't *walk;* he ambles....

The more Curb talked—and the drowsier he became—the more I detected faint traces of an accent that seemed southern or southwestern. ("Contemporary," for example, was beginning to come out "kin-timp-rary.") This reminded me that he is a product of Savannah, Georgia—he was born there on Christmas Eve, 1944—and so I changed the subject and asked him to fill me in on his childhood.

"My parents now live in Pittsburgh," he said, "but before that we lived for a long time in Oklahoma City and also in Los Angeles. We left Savannah when I was four. I went to Grant High School in Los Angeles, and for two years to San Fernando Valley State College. My father's a lawyer, and he raised me to go into law. I spent a lot of time with him and his business associates, and I think that's been of great value in terms of being able to deal with adults.

"The record business is like any other business. You are dealing with adults. The major distributors are adults and the major retail outlets are controlled by adults. Even though young people are making a tremendous contribution to the creative side of music, the idea of displaying hatred for anyone over thirty, as so many young people do, only destroys the communication lines to expose your product. Young people are dependent on adults in many ways, so they'd better learn how to communicate with them. I've tried to do that, and certainly my relationship with my father aided me."...

Curb was still droopy-eyed, and I knew he faced an afternoon of appointments, so I moved quickly through a few final questions. He told me that he was a bachelor and lived with his sister in a "contemporary, uncluttered, homey," four-bedroom house in Trousdale, "in the hills of Beverly Hills." He had a chauffeur, and entertained mostly in connection with business. "We have receptions at the house for our artists, or we have the company's foreign representatives come out when they're in town," he told me....

As for financial success, it had made little change in his way of life: "I have yet to spend a dime. I haven't gotten into investments, and I really haven't had a chance to think much about personal expenditure."

As for the future: He was developing a Broadway musical, and his friends predicted that someday he would go into politics.

DUDLEY J. LE BLANC

℞ for Millions

Inheritance, hard work, luck—there are a lot of paths to the coveted status of the millionaire. But no one's ever found a pot of gold at the end of a rainbow. Or have they? According to Paul Sann, Dudley J. LeBlanc found a magic elixir whose secret formula changed a down-and-out burial insurance salesman into a king.

Now one is reminded (hic) of the beautiful binge that went by the name of Hadacol back in 1950. In that banner year, State Senator Dudley J. LeBlanc of Louisiana, who invented the stuff, hauled in 24 million dollars, most of it from his own neighbors in the Cajun country and its environs. The wonder is that the portly little politician didn't do even better, because Hadacol happened to be more like a cocktail (make it two cocktails, and see what the boys in the back room will have) than a patent medicine. What the Senator stirred up in that barrel in his barn, using a boat oar, was a very special blend of vitamins, minerals, honey and just plain ethyl alcohol—12 percent alcohol, pal. Dudley LeBlanc was no piker when it came to mixing. He wasn't exactly stupid, either. With

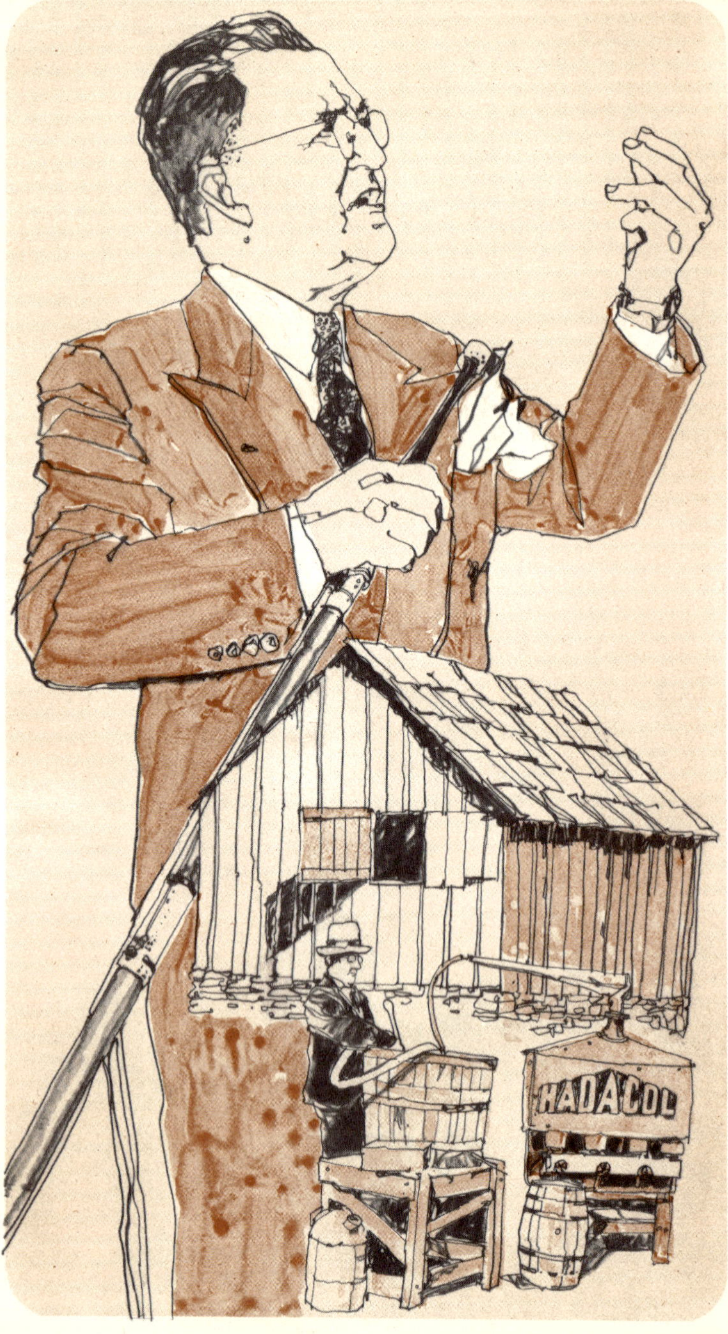
HADACOL

that high alcoholic content, he had himself a remedy laced with a strong appeal for the Bible Belt, where a man with a real thirst had no place to turn but to the sometimes elusive moonshiner.

You see, you could get yourself a little edge with Hadacol, or you could take it for what the testimonials said: anemia, arthritis, asthma, diabetes, eczema, epilepsy, gallstones, hay fever, heart trouble, high blood pressure (or low, for that matter), rheumatism, cancer, paralytic strokes, pellagra, pneumonia, tuberculosis or them naggin' ulcers....

The Senator was something more than a medicine man, of course. He was a supersalesman. Born in the time of the Puritans, he would have peddled the first firewater to the Indians. Plunked down on a farm in French-speaking Vermillion Parish in southern Louisiana in 1894, son of the penny-poor village smithy and barefoot till he was ready for primary school in Erath, he pointed himself toward the world of commerce at an early age. He sold things people needed: tobacco, patent medicines, burial insurance. He was such a good tobacco salesman that he was able to put four brothers through college, in his footsteps, on the proceeds. After that, following a stint in the Army, he peddled patent medicines and then went into burial insurance (one dollar a month and we'll take care of the body). Operating his own company, he nailed down 200,000 subscribers so fast that he was able to sell out for a neat $320,000, only to lose the bundle in the mild stock market tumble of 1937....

Couzin Dud didn't quit there. No, sir. The ills of his own flesh prompted him to stay in the therapeutic service of the people. Stricken with rheumatism, in 1943, he enjoyed some relief from a Vitamin B complex and proceeded to dig into the pharmaceutical manuals to find out what his doctor knew....

He goes into hock for $2,500 for the raw materials, rolls up his sleeves, disappears into his barn, flicks on the weak overhead lamp, finds an empty barrel that's reasonably antiseptic, and puts his fleshy shoulder to the aforementioned oar. Hour after endless hour, pouring sweat in the choking heat of the Louisiana night (where's that damn Gulf-borne breeze?), he toils to bring succor to his fellowman. A touch of thiamin hydrochloride (B1) and riboflavin (B2), a spot of niacin, a dash of pyridoxine (B6) and pantothenic acid. A spot of likker. A sprinkling of iron, manganese, calcium and phosphorous. A taste of honey. Another jigger of booze to loosen up the mixture. Hmnn. The old ethyl ain't Bourbon but it sure is more than a preservative. It goes down kinda nice.

And so the Senator comes out of the barn with

Hadacol, high-octane Hadacol. Good for all your parts, it is perforce the ideal product for Dudley LeBlanc's Happy Day Company.

Happy days, indeed, were right around the corner.

...He put the show on the road, like the circus. Never mind the freaks and the animal acts. LeBlanc got himself some headline names and organized the Hadacol Good Will Caravan. Names? You might see Mickey Rooney ("Andy Hardy uses Hadacol"), Burns and Allen, Chico Marx, Connee Boswell, Carmen Miranda, Jack Dempsey belting a stiff around in an exhibition, maybe Bob Hope or Jimmy Durante on a quick one-shot (if you'll pardon the expression) for Dudley LeBlanc's cure-all....

...Couzin Dud also used the magazines and a thousand billboards or so...moving all the way up to a $75,000 network special with Groucho Marx in Los Angeles in an abortive effort to float Hadacol out of the provinces and into the big time. On that show, Marx asked the Hadacol King, known more locally as the King of the Cajuns in his less affluent days, what his bottled elixir was good for. "It was good for five and a half million for me last year," the Senator said.

MRS. STUYVESANT FISH

Laughing All the Way

Among the grande dames of Newport high society, there was no more blithe spirit than Mrs. Stuyvesant Fish. At her beautiful home "Crossways," Mamie Fish entertained on a grand and eccentric scale. Once she gave a dinner for a foreign "prince," who turned out to be a monkey in evening dress. After enjoying several glasses of champagne, the monkey clambered up on Mrs. Fish's huge chandelier and began pelting the guests with light bulbs. Never a dull moment at home with Mrs. Fish, says society biographer Cleveland Amory.

Mrs. Belmont was the *grande dame* of Newport's Golden Age but Mrs. Fish was its *enfant terrible*.... For a lady who was by no means beautiful, who had only, as she herself put it, "a few million," and who cared little for art or theater and less for music or literature, to accomplish such a feat was remarkable enough. It was more remarkable since Mrs. Fish never went to school, could not spell even the simplest words, rarely read even a newspaper, and, if she could manage to scrawl a dash-littered letter, she could not, if her life depended on it, make such a letter legible. She had,

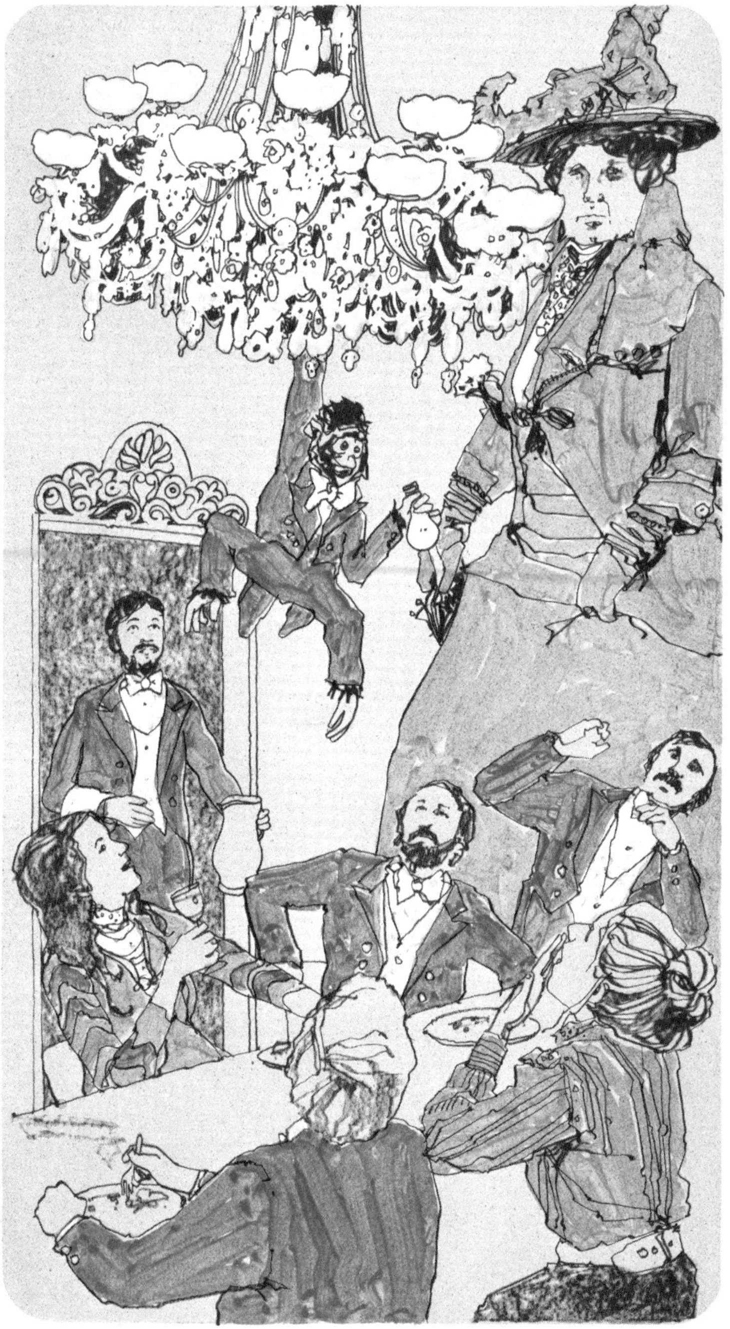

however, two vital assets, a quick wit and a sharp tongue, and with these went a large ambition. As she once told her daughter-in-law, "It doesn't make any difference what you decide to do in life, but you must do it better than anyone else." Mrs. Fish chose to be a hostess, and today, looking back, even her enemies agree that more people had more fun on more occasions *chez* Mrs. Fish than they had anywhere else. In the bargain, it went without saying, they would be insulted. That was to be expected; it was Mrs. Fish's way. Disliking the era in which she lived, she chose to spend her life making fun of it, and a vital part of her own having fun was making fun of others. In the end, the lady who could hardly write her own name not only wrote a new chapter in American society but also became, of the old era, perhaps its greatest satirist....

...Rebelling at the two- and even three-hour dinners of the times, Mrs. Fish had them served in fifty, or even forty, minutes. Her record was an eight-course dinner in thirty minutes flat. At this dinner footmen were so anxious to meet the deadline that participants recalled it was necessary to hold the plate down with one hand and eat with the other. Elisha Dyer, during the fish course, took a bone from his mouth and by the time he put it down, the meat course was in front of him. Mrs. Fish's other dining innovation was the serving of champagne, in preference to wine, from the oysters on. "You have to liven these people up," she said. "Wine just makes them sleepy."

Mrs. Fish's greetings to her guests were as unique as her service. "Howdy-do, howdy-do," she would say impatiently, pushing the newly arrived guests at Mr. Fish with a look of keen annoyance. "Make yourselves at home," she would add. "And believe me, there is no one who wishes you were there more than I do." One guest had a special greeting. "Oh," said Mrs. Fish, surprised, "I'd quite forgotten I asked you." The conclusions of her parties were equally curious. One guest made an excuse to leave early. "I promised I would be home by..." he began. "Don't apologize," broke in Mrs. Fish. "No guest ever left too soon for me." Once bored with one of her own parties, she had the orchestra play "Home, Sweet Home" before the guests' carriages had even been called. An enthusiastic beau begged for one more two-step. "There are just two steps more for you," said Mrs. Fish, "one upstairs to get your coat and the other out to your carriage."...Ladies' luncheons were her particular bêtes noires. "Here you all are," she said greeting one, "older faces and younger clothes." At another time she gave a luncheon for fifty ladies and through it all sat upstairs, refusing to come down. Finally her maid begged her at least to come down and say good-by. "But, Mrs. Fish," she said, "you invited them two weeks ago." Mrs. Fish waved her maid away. "Tell them I've changed my mind," she said.

On an individual scale Mrs. Fish's insults were even more cherished—though she never could remember names and addressed everyone as "Pet" or "Sweet pet," "Lamb" or "Sweet lamb." She was particularly acid on the favored feminine topic of babies. A lady asked her, concerning a large and constantly expanding Newport family, if she had seen Mrs. So-and-so's last baby. "Pet," replied Mrs. Fish, "I don't expect to live that long." ...On the question of house guests she was particularly outspoken. Even Harry Lehr, who served her as court chamberlain as Ward McAllister had Mrs. Astor, was not above occasional reproach. One day after his marriage to Mrs. Dahlgren, a group at "Crossways" were trying to guess each other's favorite flower. "I know Mamie's," said Lehr quickly, "the climbing rose." Mrs. Fish smiled. "And I yours, pet," she replied, "the marigold." One day Lehr introduced her to the Englishman Tony Shaw Safe who had come to the resort as manager of a polo team and stayed on to marry a wealthy Newporter and hyphenate his name from Shaw Safe to Shaw-Safe. He was particularly insistent on being called by the full hyphenation. "Howdy-do, Mr. Safe," Mrs. Fish blithely greeted him. "I'm so sorry to call you Mr. Safe but I've forgotten your combination."...

...With other members of Newport's Great Triumvirate Mrs. Fish feuded with equal aplomb. One day at the Newport Casino Mrs. Belmont swept up to her. "I have just heard what you said about me at Tessie Oelrichs' last night. You cannot deny it, Mamie, because Tessie told me herself. You told everybody I looked like a frog." Mrs. Fish was alarmed. "No, no," she said. "Not a frog! A toad, my pet, a *toad!*"

...On her invitation cards she would scrawl in her illegible hand, "There will be something besides the dinner, come." There always was—and people always came. It might be Crown Prince William of Sweden or it might be a series of vaudeville acts, it might be Irene Castle or it might be John L. Sullivan, it might be the chorus of "The Merry Widow" or it might be a ballroom full of live butterflies. One thing was certain; it would be fun.

Texas tycoons Clint Murchison and Sid Richardson once wagered an even $1 million on the turn of a card. (Murchison lost.)

Electrical-Contracting Co.
SHARES

JIMMY LING

Profile of a Wheeler-Dealer

He had a twenty-room mansion with a bomb shelter personally designed by physicist Edward Teller, a vest pocket golf course and a lot of brass. The man was James Joseph Ling, who started a $3.75 billion empire at the Texas State Fair. Impossible? Not for Jimmy Ling, wheeler-dealer par excellence. Check this 1967 Newsweek *account of the life and times of this merger king.*

It wasn't long ago that Dallas oilmen and other pillars of the Texas Establishment had an instant formula for a barrel of laughs: just mention the name of Jimmy Ling. In air-cooled private clubs 40 floors above the sun-blasted streets, the tycoons would sink into their deep, brown-cowhide chairs, sip twenty-year-old bourbon and poke a little fun at the rising young corporate merger artist from Hugo, Okla.

"I just won't do business with a Chinaman," one oilman would chortle. "Did you hear?" a second would ask. "He's going to take over Bell Telephone next." "What's he going to call it," a third would ask, "Ting-a-Ling?"

No one laughs at James Joseph Ling any more. To be sure, 44-year-old Ling has not managed to buy Ma Bell—not yet. But he has staged one of the greatest exhibitions of financial legerdemain and managerial acumen in the post-World War II era. In one short decade, he has dazzled Dallas and Wall Street alike by piling merger upon merger, parlaying a modest, $2 million-a-year electrical-contracting business into today's $1.8 billion Ling-Temco-Vought Inc.

This year alone, Ling's LTV acquired the sprawling, $1 billion Wilson & Co. (meat packing, sports equipment, drugs) and concluded a deal to acquire the $500 million Greatamerica Corp. (insurance and Braniff International Airways).... From his brand-new, 33-story LTV tower in downtown Dallas, Jimmy Ling, the son of an oil-field laborer, presided last week over what experts believe to be the fastest growing major company in the world. Expected sales of $1.8 billion this year (vs. only $468 million last year) are more than 400 times greater than LTV's sales back in 1957; profits are up 400-fold, and investors who bought 100 shares of Ling stock ten years ago at $2 a share would have stock that is worth about $20,000 today.

The man who worked this miracle looks more like a pro football quarterback than a business genius. Daily workouts hold his powerful, 6-foot 2-inch frame down to a tightly muscled 200 pounds and he walks with the spring of an athlete.

He once wore stylish Continental suits and roll-collar shirts. Now, in deference to the more conservative image he wants to project as the captain of a giant enterprise, the suits run to faultlessly tailored Ivy League cuts and the shirts are buttoned down.

When Ling talks, however, all doubts about his calling vanish. At the approach of an inquiring outsider, Ling shoots from his chair as if spring-propelled, extends a powerful hand, fixes the caller intently with his piercing black eyes, and begins a tireless, nonstop explanation of his methods and his goals. He refutes criticism before it is voiced, ticks off points on his fingers—all the while spewing out dates, facts and figures in his earnest Southwestern drawl. His speech, reflecting his blunt competitive drive, is laced with jargon from the world of sports and the military. He talks of "Project Redeployment," of "Project Touchdown," of an "end run" he pulled to achieve a certain goal. His plans are bound by "conservative parameters," he sustains "a karate chop" when things go wrong. People who stand in his way are guilty of "overkill."

... The company Ling has created turns out products that range from hamburgers to missiles, from steel tennis rackets to radio antennas, from electrical cable and drugs to jet bombers (the Navy's A-7). It is thus a classic example of the widely diversified, so-called conglomerate corporation—and the construction of such sprawling new conglomerates is the hottest game in U.S. business today....

What kind of men does it take to pull off the big deals? Men with brains and guts, certainly, plus other attributes they tend to share. One is an infinite capacity for hard work. Ling thinks his own 90-hour workweek not at all extraordinary.

Ling's mother died when he was 12 and he was sent to live with an aunt in Louisiana. He did six years of schoolwork in three years by going to classes year round, but before graduating from high school, Ling grew bored with studies and quit. He bummed around the country for four years, then entered the Navy during World War II and served as an electrician.

After the war, Ling founded an electrical-contracting business and was soon making a handsome living. But it was small potatoes to Jimmy, who by now was thinking very big and studying annual reports and business trade journals with intense interest. "The task was to get past understanding," Ling recalls, "and look for applications."

In the upshot, Ling decided to go public, an unconventional move for an electrical contractor. He penned his own stock prospectus, had a lawyer "sprinkle holy water on it," and with a fine disregard for orthodoxy hawked the shares himself door-to-door and at a booth at the Texas State Fair. Dallas businessmen laughed in his face, and started telling the "Chinaman" joke (his name actually is Bavarian). "Those were tough times," snaps Ling, "our purgatory days." But the issue sold, and months later, Ling pulled off his first acquisition and was on board the merger escalator.

Postscript

In 1970 James Ling's merger escalator ground to a halt and subsequently slid precipitately into reverse. After economic recession and antitrust suits, LTV stock plummeted from 169 1/2 to 10. Ling was booted out. Today, unconquerable as chewing gum, Ling is back on top, boss of Omega-Alpha, literally the "son of LTV," following in its sire's footsteps with annual sales of about $225 million.

J. PAUL GETTY

The World Is Mean to Millionaires

Gold diggers, panhandlers, greed and hostility everywhere—such is the view from the top, according to J. Paul Getty, perhaps the world's wealthiest human being. Contrary to popular belief, Getty feels, a rich man's lot is not a happy one.

Never have the burdens of wealth been greater than they are today, and never have its rewards been slimmer. Rich people once lived in a world apart; today almost the only difference between the multimillionaire and the reasonably well-to-do man earning $15,000 to $25,000 a year is that the millionaire works harder, relaxes less, is burdened with greater responsibilities and is exposed to the constant glare of publicity.

The greatest difference lies in the exposure to publicity. As soon as this is published, I know my mail will increase from an average low of 50 letters a day to 300, 400 or even 1,000. My two secretaries will be working overtime for weeks dealing with long letters from complete strangers, usually written in crabbed, almost indecipherable handwriting, and headed "Dear Paul"—so that they *might* conceivably be from old friends, long lost sight of....A few, like one I received recently, will demand "one million dollars by return mail since you have so much of the stuff."...

I want to make it clear that I don't resent this state of affairs. I accept it as part of the penalty of being rich and known....

But this is not to say that I am indifferent to all the unwanted attention. Indeed, it often annoys me. Perhaps it's the lack of consideration of the well-to-do solicitors for charities that irks me most: It doesn't seem to occur to these people that I, too, have charities I'm interested in, and that I'd never dare to do indiscriminate fundraising among acquaintances of mine, let alone total strangers. As Groucho Marx once said, in an unforgettable hotel-lobby scene: "Boy, what are you shouting my name for? Do I go around shouting your name?"...

I first became aware of the penalties of being rich when my father died....The size of his estate was commented on in the press....My mother, Sarah Catharine Getty, his widow, then aged 78, received hundreds of proposals of marriage from total strangers from all over the world. Acquaintances who had never paid particular attention to me would come up and say, "You related to that rich oil man who died the other day?" When I explained, they'd say, "You mean to say he was your *father?*" and I could see in their eyes a sinister glint that hadn't been there before....

I disagree, now more than ever, with Scott Fitzgerald's often-quoted remark to Ernest Hemingway: "The rich are different from us."...

Since multimillionaires have been stripped of so many status symbols and must live very much as other people do, they should, I think, be entitled to the same courtesies. If I go to a doctor, I should be charged the regular fee. If I go to a hotel, I should pay the standard charge for a room. And when I tip, I shouldn't be expected to tip more than the average man. It's rude and inconsiderate to overtip. It only makes things difficult—and embarrassing—for people who are not as rich as I am....

... There was this business of the pay phone I had installed in my country house in England to be used by my guests. When *I'm* staying with friends and have to make long-distance calls, I make a point of making them from a pay phone in the nearest town or village. I had the pay phone installed in my place because I knew that guests preferred it that way. It saved them the trouble of settling with me afterward, or of attempting to pay for their phone calls. It saved them trouble. And yet a spate of letters and cartoons resulted. You might have thought I was pathologically inclined, instead of taking the simple, rational step.

Just as a millionaire has to be wary about hangers-on, he has to be wary about the feminine company he keeps. This is where the rich man is penalized enormously for being rich. The penalty he pays for divorce makes many a rich man unwilling to marry in the first place....

With all these problems, why bother to become a millionaire in the first place? In my case, I inherited a certain amount of wealth and was determined to use this wealth constructively. I take a certain pride in running a corporation, if not more successfully than other people, at any rate just as successfully as most....There are people, of course, who have been destroyed, physically and morally, by their wealth. The same people, born poor, would probably have become alcoholics or thieves.

Though our rewards may be small, we are, if our society is to remain in its present form, essential to the nation's prosperity. We provide others with incentives which would not exist if we were to disappear. As active businessmen, we find it useful to have money simply because a tolerable margin of financial security makes for increased efficiency and competitiveness. If I were not using my fortune usefully, I would have little justification for having it in the first place. And if you then took it away, it wouldn't make all that much difference to me. At least I wouldn't be getting all those letters.

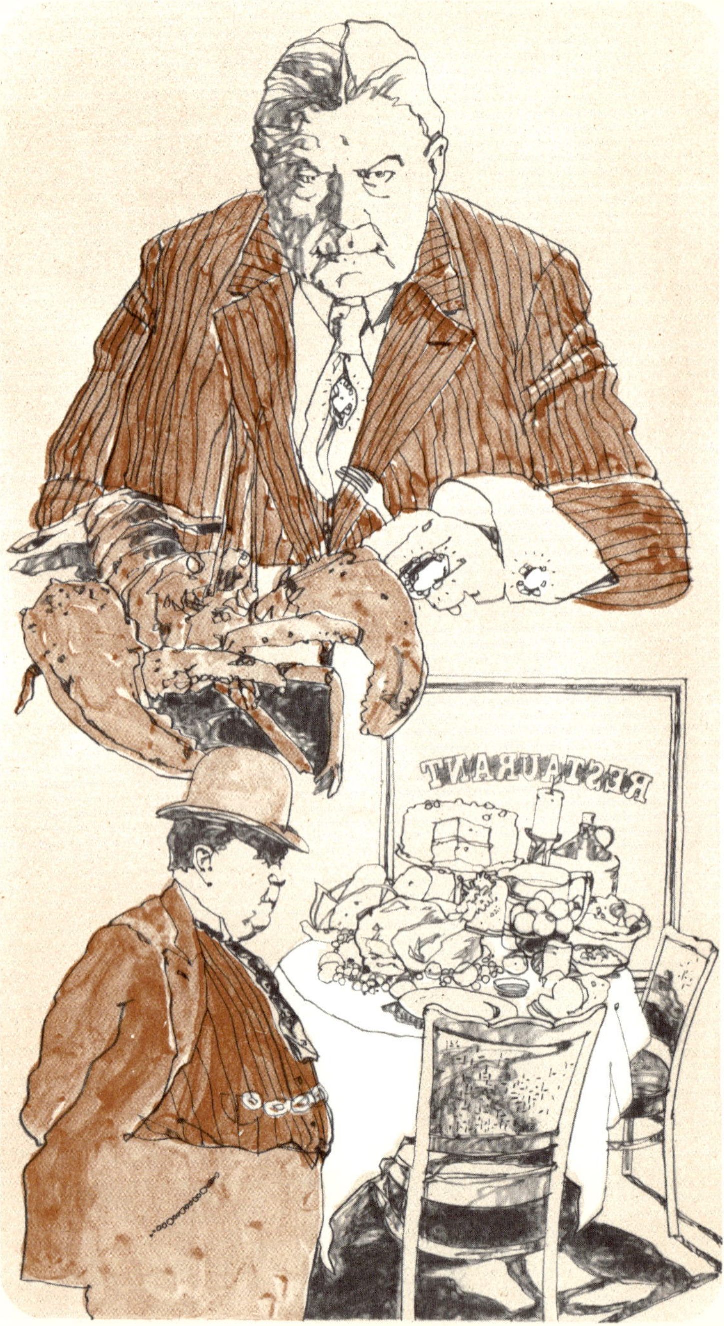
RESTAURANT

"DIAMOND JIM" BRADY

King of the Gay White Way

No man better symbolizes the flaunting of great wealth than James Buchanan Brady. Even today his name is synonymous with spendthrift philandering. Truly he was a gem of the Gilded Age.

"Diamond Jim" Brady had a unique, official position in the world of Broadway. People called him the king of the Gay White Way, though actually he held multiple posts and exercised powers that far exceeded those of his purely decorative royalty. He was Broadway's master of revels, its oracle and arbiter, its greatest host, its premier angel and philanthropist, its outstanding playboy, its most benevolent, authoritative pander. All America knew James Buchanan Brady by sight as well as reputation—he had seen to that. A master of personal publicity, he had purposefully made himself a living legend. The son of a West Street saloon keeper, thrown on his own resources in childhood, without formal education and almost illiterate, Brady had become a multimillionaire. He was a supersalesman of railroad equipment, and an unusually successful Wall Street speculator. His fortune was rated at twelve million, his annual income at one million. Reproached by George Rector for being a soft touch, for letting himself be trimmed by sycophants, male and female, Brady replied gravely, "Being a sucker is fun—if you can afford it." It was much the same with his gaudy sets of enormous gems—he had thirty sets, each composed of twenty items, and collectively they included more than twenty thousand diamonds, of varying size and shape, as well as six thousand other precious stones. Decked out in one of his matching sets of jewels, Brady looked like an excursion steamer at twilight. "Them as has 'em, wears 'em," he explained. His jewels, his prodigal spending, his uncouth manner, his sulphurous private life flagrantly exposed to public view were elements of an apparatus of publicity that returned enormous profits.

"Diamond Jim" even exploited his monstrous aspect, his gargantuan appetite. He tipped the scales at nearly two hundred and fifty pounds; his majestic stomach began at his collar bone, beneath triple chins, and swelled in an opulent curve toward his massive legs. His huge purple-red face was chiefly remarkable for a pair of small, close-set, shrewd porcine eyes, a heavy, undershot, pugnacious jaw with bulldog jowls. Buried in that ugly flesh was a kindly, boyish smile. "Diamond Jim" did not smoke, nor did he consume any alcohol; his favorite drink was freshly squeezed orange juice, of which he often swallowed four gallons during a meal. He was a marathon eater. George Rector described him as "the best twenty-five customers we had." Wilson Mizner, a playboy who had connections with the criminal underworld and achieved Broadway celebrity as a wit, said that Brady liked his oysters sprinkled with clams, and his steaks smothered in veal cutlets. This was hardly an exaggeration. At Rector's, with an oversize napkin tied around his neck, Brady would polish off four dozen oysters, a dozen hard-shell crabs, six or seven giant lobsters, a large steak, a tray of French pastry and coffee. "Whenever I sit down to a meal," he once said, "I always make it a point to leave just four inches between my stummick and the edge of the table. And then, when I can feel 'em rubbin' together pretty hard, I *know* I've had enough." Broadway, having its own peculiar standards, regarded "Diamond Jim" as more of a gourmet than a gourmand. It also considered him a great gentleman.

Text set in Monotype Walbaum, a light, open typeface designed by Justus Erich Walbaum (1768-1839). Display type set in Embassy Script and a Shaded Engravers' Roman, designed in the mid-nineteenth century by David Wolf Bruce. Printed on Hallmark Eggshell Book paper. Designed by Richard S. Peterson.